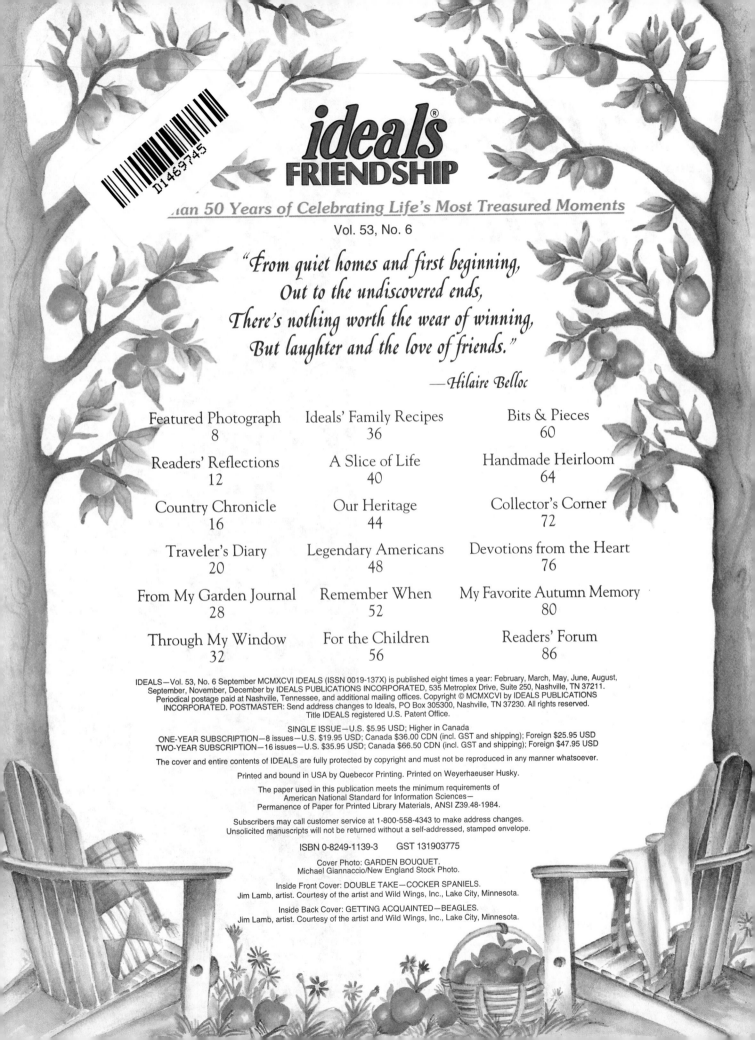

ideals® FRIENDSHIP

...an 50 Years of Celebrating Life's Most Treasured Moments

Vol. 53, No. 6

"From quiet homes and first beginning,
Out to the undiscovered ends,
There's nothing worth the wear of winning,
But laughter and the love of friends."

—Hilaire Belloc

IDEALS—Vol. 53, No. 6 September MCMXCVI IDEALS (ISSN 0019-137X) is published eight times a year: February, March, May, June, August, September, November, December by IDEALS PUBLICATIONS INCORPORATED, 535 Metroplex Drive, Suite 250, Nashville, TN 37211. Periodical postage paid at Nashville, Tennessee, and additional mailing offices. Copyright © MCMXCVI by IDEALS PUBLICATIONS INCORPORATED. POSTMASTER: Send address changes to Ideals, PO Box 305300, Nashville, TN 37230. All rights reserved. Title IDEALS registered U.S. Patent Office.

SINGLE ISSUE—U.S. $5.95 USD; Higher in Canada
ONE-YEAR SUBSCRIPTION—8 issues—U.S. $19.95 USD; Canada $36.00 CDN (incl. GST and shipping); Foreign $25.95 USD
TWO-YEAR SUBSCRIPTION—16 issues—U.S. $35.95 USD; Canada $66.50 CDN (incl. GST and shipping); Foreign $47.95 USD

Printed and bound in USA by Quebecor Printing. Printed on Weyerhaeuser Husky.

The paper used in this publication meets the minimum requirements of
American National Standard for Information Sciences—
Permanence of Paper for Printed Library Materials, ANSI Z39.48-1984.

Subscribers may call customer service at 1-800-558-4343 to make address changes.
Unsolicited manuscripts will not be returned without a self-addressed, stamped envelope.

ISBN 0-8249-1139-3   GST 131903775

Cover Photo: GARDEN BOUQUET.
Michael Giannaccio/New England Stock Photo.

Inside Front Cover: DOUBLE TAKE—COCKER SPANIELS.
Jim Lamb, artist. Courtesy of the artist and Wild Wings, Inc., Lake City, Minnesota.

Inside Back Cover: GETTING ACQUAINTED—BEAGLES.
Jim Lamb, artist. Courtesy of the artist and Wild Wings, Inc., Lake City, Minnesota.

Autumn Rapture

George R. Kossik

I, when the summer was over,
Found autumn was covered with gold;
And colors more lovely than springtime
Were there for these eyes to behold.

Lost in a sweet fascination,
I gazed on with wonder and awe
Then, rapt in serene adoration,
Praised God in the glory I saw.

HEWETT'S CORNERS
Vermont
Gene Ahrens Photography

Nature's Patchwork Shawl

Loise Pinkerton Fritz

The moon shines down upon the trees,
　　Upon the late, late summer leaves,
With golden-mellowed, gentle beams.
　　Soon summer will fade like a dream.

Green meadows, forests, fields, and hills
　　Will feel the touch of autumn's chill
As Jack Frost, with his brush in hand,
　　Expertly tints autumnal lands.

'Tis true we love the summer so,
　　Its sunshine and soft moonbeam glow,
But oh, the beauty of the fall
　　When Nature wears its patchwork shawl.

New Carpet

Dean Robbins

The carpet man was here last night
But never came indoors.
Instead he found the tree out back
And carpeted the backyard floor.

I can't begrudge his workmanship,
For all is covered well.
No seams or gaps are visible;
No fraying edges I can tell.

And colors? They are plentiful—
Some earthy green and brown
With yellow and a touch of red.
A fall mosaic he put down.

A job well done, as good work goes;
And yet, I must complain.
What self-respecting carpet man
Would leave his product for the rain?

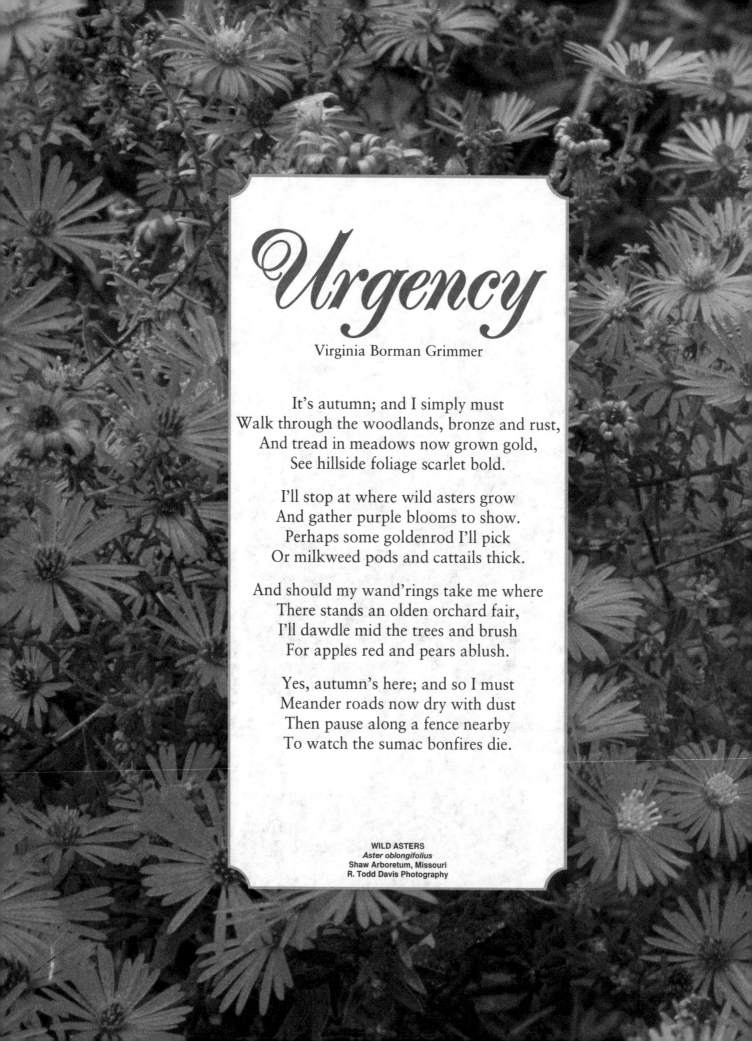

Urgency

Virginia Borman Grimmer

It's autumn; and I simply must
Walk through the woodlands, bronze and rust,
And tread in meadows now grown gold,
See hillside foliage scarlet bold.

I'll stop at where wild asters grow
And gather purple blooms to show.
Perhaps some goldenrod I'll pick
Or milkweed pods and cattails thick.

And should my wand'rings take me where
There stands an olden orchard fair,
I'll dawdle mid the trees and brush
For apples red and pears ablush.

Yes, autumn's here; and so I must
Meander roads now dry with dust
Then pause along a fence nearby
To watch the sumac bonfires die.

WILD ASTERS
Aster oblongifolius
Shaw Arboretum, Missouri
R. Todd Davis Photography

Readers' Reflections

GOD'S WORLD

I walked down nature's trail today
And felt the autumn chill.
The vibrant leaves of red and gold
Embraced each vale and hill.

The gentle breeze was singing
While playing through the trees;
The tiny blooms were fading
As they were kissed by bees.

The leaves were gently falling,
And they hated to let go;
But they knew the time was coming
When they'd taste the winter's snow.

This is the only proof I need
That God is in command—
When I see the seasons changing
Across our wondrous land.

Who else could cause the trees to blaze
Or bring the mystic snow,
Could put the rainbow in the sky
Or make the flowers grow?

You may not have much wealth on earth;
You may be weak and old;
But nature's beauty is worth more
Than pockets full of gold.

Margie Kinard
Gastonia, North Carolina

AUTUMN

As I drive along a country road,
The trees are dressed, so bold
In scarlet, beige, and russet,
In yellow and glistening gold.

Drying cornstalks standing tall
Silhouette against an autumn sky;

Orange pumpkins dot the fields
Soon to be picked for a holiday pie.

Deep within my memory
These sights I shall recall
On cold and dreary winter days—
The wonderful colors of fall!

Gertrude Dunham
Bloomfield, New Jersey

PRELUDE TO AUTUMN

The summer now is ending,
And nights are getting cold.
The autumn thus is nearing
As time is growing old.

Now God, the Master Painter,
Will paint in vibrant shades
The trees high on the mountains
And those in forest glades.

My heart with joy is singing
As I hear the songbird call,
And I see the pumpkins ripening
Along the garden wall.

The apples too are swaying
So gently in the breeze.
I see the farmer walking
To survey his boundaries.

And gazing at his harvest,
He offers thanks to God.
There's a light within the window
As homeward now he trods.

I'm thankful too for blessings
That God has sent my way.
I hear the church bells pealing,
And I too pause to pray.

For I have friends who love me,
A rooftop o'er my head,
A house all warm and cozy,
And gifts of daily bread.

I feel deep down within me
Such joy and peace untold;
I too have reaped a harvest
Worth more than shining gold.

Mary E. Randall Herrington
Phoenix, Arizona

LEAVES

Oh, look! The leaves of gold and brown
Are swirling, twirling, coming down.
The wind is shaking every bough.
The ground is nearly covered now.

Let's rake them up from where they lie;
We'll pile them till they're ten feet high.
We'll climb onto that branch up there
And both come flying through the air.

We'll hear that lovely swooshing sound
As we and leaves come sliding down;
All afternoon we'll climb and leap
Into these leaves we've piled so deep.

When all the leaves have tumbled down,
We'll gather twigs from all around;
We'll build a bonfire big and bright
And toast marshmallows here tonight.

These autumn leaves will smell so good
Combined with scents of burning wood;
We'll sing around the flickering fire
While I strum on my old guitar.

We'll see the moon rise in the sky,
Watch shooting stars, and wonder why
These fun-filled days must disappear
And why fall comes just once a year.

We'll laugh and talk till almost dawn;
With heavy eyes we'll start to yawn.
We'll make up beds from fallen leaves
And sleep all day beneath these trees.

Cherri Franks-Turnbull
Albuquerque, New Mexico

This Fair Autumn Day

John C. Bonser

When bright October lifts its golden arms in crisp salutes
To autumn's patched-quilt hills and clear and tranquil sky,
I leave familiar highways and their faster, well-used routes
For country roads that lead to yesterdays gone by.

I pass by once-red barns whose peeling paint reveals their plight
And by green-shuttered, frame farmhouses, aging too,
Whose owners' sunburned brows grew furrowed as their hair turned white
And daily chores became more difficult to do.

I drive through ancient, little towns where nothing seems to stir,
Not even old hound dogs still sleeping in the sun;
Where Time itself, immune to unimportant speed, confers
Its laurels on all these whose races have been run.

The nearby woods are vainly clinging to their amber leaves
In hopes the winter will not bury them in snow;
Squirrels are scurrying to store acorns in sheltered eaves
While tiny sparrows overhead flit to and fro.

There is a sadness in the beauty of such solitude
That in no way detracts from this fair autumn day—
When for a few brief hours, I now am able to intrude
On scenes the winds of change lack strength to blow away!

Country CHRONICLE
Lansing Christman

FINDING AN OLD FRIEND

I felt a comfortable familiarity the other day, like shaking hands with an old friend, when I took the old grass scythe down from the pegs that had held it to a beam in the barn. It had been there, untouched, for the past fifty years, gathering dust and spider webs. It was an old scythe, and I was an old man too.

Actually I just wanted to test again my skill at using a scythe. My father taught me the art when I was a boy. As farmers, we always cut the weeds and brush that sprang up along stonewalls, wild weeds bent on usurping the productive soil of the meadows and fields.

Then when I gave up farming, I hung the scythe in the barn and let the bushes grow. The chokecherries grew freely once again and were food for the birds. (I even ate some of the dark, puckery fruit now and then; there wasn't much taste.) Sumac always bore its lovely scarlet leaves along the stone walls every fall, and the leaves of Virginia creeper turned a dark, deep red.

When I took hold of the handle of the scythe, I felt the touch of an old friend, kind and smooth, warm and almost affectionate. I used a whetstone to sharpen the blade and went to work on a road bank. The grass and weeds fell evenly as the sharp, keen blade swept through their paths. I had no real need to use the scythe; I just wanted to get the feel again of the handles on the curved wooden shaft to which the blade was attached, and I wanted to test the strength of my arms and hands, older now by fifty years.

I learned something more that day, something more than meeting an old friend. I learned that knowing and remembering the old ways on the farm kept me close to the soil, and I have an inner feeling that my closeness to the earth keeps my beating heart more in rhythm to God's world.

The author of two published books, Lansing Christman has been contributing to Ideals *for more than twenty years. Mr. Christman has also been published in several American, foreign, and braille anthologies. He lives in rural South Carolina.*

Corn Cadets

Darlene Christianson

Stalks of corn
Wait in the dusk,
Their ears adorned
With silken husk.

Tassel-topped,
Erect they stand,
Listening for
The wind's command.

Rustling softly,
Standing proudly,
Then marching stiffly,
Clapping loudly—

Tall, impressive
Silhouettes
Of ripe and ready
Corn cadets.

AUTUMN HARVEST
Plain, Wisconsin
Ken Dequaine Photography

TRAVELER'S
Diary

Pearl Landon

Friday morning, late September
Bennington, Vermont

Our autumn tour of northern New England began yesterday in Bennington, Vermont. We were up with the first light to begin our tour of this historic city nestled in Vermont's southwestern corner. The calendar says September, but with frost on the grass and our breath visible in the air, the morning felt more like November. The bright, blue sky promised a sunny, comfortable afternoon, however; so we threw our sweaters over our shoulders and were on our way.

We walked first to the Old First Church in Monument Circle. With its clean, square lines and bright white clapboards, the church is classic New England— a beautiful example of colonial architecture. In the cemetery outside the church, we met a young couple on a literary pilgrimage of sorts. They had driven from Boston to visit the poet Robert Frost's grave site, which we discovered amid the graves of colonial and British soldiers who died in the Revolutionary War.

From the church, we walked north up Monument Avenue to the Bennington Battle Monument. The striking granite spire stands atop a hill overlooking the Walloomsac River. The monument commemorates the Battle of Bennington, a turning point in the Revolutionary War. Its blue-gray limestone stood out in sharp contrast to the reds, yellows, and golds of the surrounding countryside.

Tonight we prepare for an early morning departure and an entire week of autumn sightseeing in Vermont and New Hampshire; I wonder, however, if anything to come will match the view we had today in Bennington.

OLD FIRST CHURCH
Bennington, Vermont
Gene Ahrens Photography

Unharvested

Robert Frost

A scent of ripeness from over a wall.
And come to leave the routine road
And look for what had made me stall,
There sure enough was an apple tree
That had eased itself of its summer load,
And of all but its trivial foliage free,
Now breathed as light as a lady's fan.
For there there had been an apple fall
As complete as the apple had given man.
The ground was one circle of solid red.

May something go always unharvested!
May much stay out of our stated plan,
Apples or something forgotten and left,
So smelling their sweetness would be no theft.

God Loves You

Minnie Klemme

Do you know how much God loves you?
Count the stars and all their kin,
Breathe the fresh air from the mountains,
Walk where winter snows have been,
Smell the flowers of the valley,
Taste the berries on the hill,
Feel the sunlight and the showers,
Listen to the wind grow still.

Do you know how much God loves you?
Watch a little child at play,
Touch the soft cheeks of a baby,
Hear a bird at close of day,
See the smile of someone dying
At a vigil's lonely end,
Know the depth of God's compassion
In the handclasp of a friend.

Love & Friendship

Emily Jane Brontë

Love is like the wild rose-briar;
 Friendship like the holly-tree.
The holly is dark when the rose-briar blooms,
 But which will bloom most constantly?

The wild rose-briar is sweet in spring;
 Its summer blossoms scent the air.
Yet wait till winter comes again,
 And who will call the wild-briar fair?

Then, scorn the silly rose-wreath now,
 And deck thee with the holly's sheen;
That, when December blights thy brow,
 He still may leave thy garland green.

From My Garden Journal

by Deana Deck

SPIDER PLANT

Once or twice a year, I spend the afternoon potting the shoots that fall gracefully from the spider plant hanging in a corner of my breakfast nook. Each "baby" is carefully transplanted into its own terra-cotta pot, soon to brighten the desk of a coworker or elate the hostess at an upcoming dinner party. I love to share plants with friends, and there is none easier to share than the spider plant (*Chlorophytum commosum 'Varigatum'*). This popular plant is also known as the airplane plant, but neither common name has ever seemed appropriate to me. *Spider* obviously refers to the shape of its babies' foliage, but it calls to mind those hardworking, but somewhat ominous-looking, scuttling critters that I keep banished to the dark, dusty corners of the garage. Chlorophytum, with its green-and-white, variegated foliage, is a clean-looking, bright-light plant that would languish in a dark corner.

I don't like the name *airplane plant* either. It sounds so techno-aluminum, all hard edges and reflective metal. The plant, in comparison, is as graceful as a vine; and to me, its gently dropping stalks with their delicate plantlets resemble tiny, wind-ruffled birds.

I think *feather plant* would be a much more appropriate name, but nobody asked me. Perhaps that's because the plant has been a household fixture for about 150 years longer than I've been around. Prior to then, it was just another exotic tropical, rarely seen out of its native South Africa.

Although spider plants are relatively carefree for houseplants, they do occasionally come down with a bout of brown leaf tips. The condition is caused by a susceptibility to high levels of soluble salts—primarily fluoride—in the potting soil. Since the plant produces the most abundant offspring when slightly root bound, repotting isn't as satisfactory a solution to the problem as simply flushing out the salts.

Fluoride and other salts find their way into the soil from the residue left behind by plant food solutions and from the fluoride in your water system. The best way to eradicate salts from the soil is to flush it with filtered water purchased from your local health food store. Most of these shops have chemical-free water on tap these days. You can take your own clean plastic jugs and fill them for anywhere from thirty to fifty cents a gallon. If you can't find a source locally, purchase a few gallons of distilled water from the supermarket.

Put the plant outdoors on a warm day, remove it from the drip tray, and flood the pot with three or four gallons of the filtered or distilled water to flush out all of the salt residue.

Let the pot sit to drain for several hours after this treatment, then water it again with a liquid plant food. This last step is important, because you will have washed out all the nutrients in the soil. If you have some clean compost handy, it wouldn't hurt to work a little into the surface of the potting soil.

I have a friend in San Diego who recently told me the spider plant is considered a ground cover in his climate, and he keeps it under control with a lawn mower. If you live in a similar climate, this method may be necessary; but to those of us in more temperate areas, it seems like a cruel fate for so lovely a plant. On the other hand, a quick snip with a mower sure sounds easy. Just about anywhere north of Miami, one has to haul the mother plant in to a comfy winter home in a sunny window and find homes for all those baby "spiders."

Making new plants for special friends from the little "feathers" or "spider babies" is quite simple, however. In fact it is almost a necessity, because you can't keep them forever. As the plant sends out the long, gently bending stalks, the plantlets that form on the end lend a full, healthy appearance to the plant; and there is always a temptation just to leave it alone. Eventually, however, those stalks will become dry and somewhat brittle; at the same time, the babies are sprouting tiny roots at their bases.

Sooner or later the plant will become impatient with you and will drop the stem—baby and all—to the ground, where in Key West or San Diego it will root quickly and live a long and happy life. In other parts of the country, however, the baby is doomed to early death by frostbite. Better you should pot it up for a pal!

The healthiest way to pot your spider plant's offspring, and one that never fails, is to pot the babies while they are still attached to the parent plant. If yours is a hanging plant, as most are, this will mean lowering it somewhat or setting it out on a picnic table or similar surface so you can surround it with small pots.

Fill each small pot with a loose mixture of potting soil and peat moss or vermiculite. Set a baby plant into each prepared pot, but do not detach it for about ten days. Then snip off the stem at both ends, close to both the parent plant and to the sprout. Put the young plants in a bright location, but avoid direct sunlight. One of the nice characteristics of the spider plant is that it will do equally well outdoors in bright light or light shade. Provide moderate light indoors. If you start new plants in the summer, you can have quite a few potted in festive containers to give as gifts by the time the holidays roll around.

Keep the plants moist, and feed them all year with liquid plant food. Use a weaker solution in winter than in summer since they require more nutrients while blooming and growing. At night they prefer fairly cool temperatures in the 50° F to 55° F range, which makes them perfectly suited to spending the winter on an enclosed porch where more tender tropicals might not thrive.

I always enjoy a quiet afternoon spent potting my spider plant's offspring; perhaps part of my joy comes from knowing the pleasure the small plants will give their new owners. For even if its name evokes images of scurrying, eight-legged creatures, I know the true beauty of this lovely, graceful plant and the joy it can bring to all my friends.

Deana Deck tends to her flowers, plants, and vegetables at her home in Nashville, Tennessee, where her popular garden column is a regular feature in The Tennessean.

Autumn in a Jar

Dorothy Evelyn Begg

Grapes ripen in the woods today
Like blue pearls in the sun;
Along stone walls and fences barbed
Their trailing tendrils run.

Around the maples in the swamp,
Across the brooks, leaf-filled,

The wild grapes drape their tender vines—
    Elixir undistilled!

The grouse, the pheasant, and the fox,
    The possum and the deer
Feast like rich kings in forest glen
    Now that September's here!

The frost has set the fragrance free,
    The scent of perfume fine—
The essence sweet of summer sun,
    Pearls strung along the vine!

The clusters shine among the leaves
    Where sumac fires are drowned;
The grouse, the deer, and small red fox
    Will winter near this mound.

And we who harvest these ripe jewels
    Brought back from woodlands far
Upon a snowy winter's day
    Find autumn in a jar.

THROUGH MY WINDOW

Pamela Kennedy

Art by Russ Flint

NEW AND IMPROVED

What is it about friends that compels them to try to improve one another? I like to believe that someone cultivates a friendship with me because she likes me the way I am. Yet I consistently find myself the target of my friends' well-intentioned remodeling schemes.

Once when we lived in Illinois, my neighbor was a delightful English woman with a penchant for garage sales and health food. I thoroughly enjoyed her instructions in bargain hunting, but less graciously accepted her relentless quest to turn me into a health food enthusiast. She dropped off "tasty treats" periodically, refusing to reveal the ingredients until I sampled them. Then she would cheerily exclaim, "See, you wouldn't know they

didn't have all that bad stuff in them, would you?" The carob Easter bonbons were okay, but I had trouble getting past the gelatinous cubes of tofu in the lasagna. In addition to her attempts at dietary modifications, she prescribed zinc for my son when she observed him biting his fingernails; and at her insistence we almost galvanized the poor kid (who, by the way, still bites his nails at age twenty-one!). One day my husband, having just ingested his first and last bite of soyburger, put a stop to her donations by standing outside her kitchen window and dramatically ingesting several candy bars.

Besides my well-meaning but unsuccessful English neighbor, I have also foiled the attempts of others who sought to broaden my horizons. In the process I have learned that I have no gifts for counted cross-stitch, Ikebana flower arranging, bridge, or gourmet Thai cooking. Still I continue to be a prime subject in the improvement plans of my acquaintances.

Recently I encountered a new friend who is an aerobics instructor. More importantly, she is an aerobics instructor who used to be overweight and out of shape. Now she's a perky size eight and is filled with a zeal that would shame a missionary. When I lamented, shortly after Christmas, that I had put on weight over the holidays and needed to trim a few pounds, she slapped a brochure in my hand and gave me her five-minute testimony on getting in shape. Before I knew what had happened, I had signed up for a twelve-week course and we were at the discount store picking out exercise clothes. As we headed for the check-out counter, she tossed a loop of terry cloth in my basket. "It's a sweatband," she announced with glee.

"Will we be doing a lot of sweating?" I inquired weakly.

"Buckets!" she affirmed with a wicked grin.

I trudged home with my bag of very small, stretchy garments and a heavy heart. Why couldn't my friends just love me, thick thighs and all?

On the first day of aerobics class, I spent a half hour getting into my gear. I was almost afraid to look in the mirror; and when I did finally venture a peek, staring back at me was something resembling a shiny, hot pink larva wearing running shoes and a sweatband. I heard a horn honk and pulled on one of my husband's old T-shirts as I dashed out to join my friend.

"All ready for the first day of the rest of your life?" she trilled as I climbed in the car.

"As ready as I'll ever be," I replied with foreboding.

The other women at the aerobics center looked like a cross-section of the fitness population. I felt better already. I was certainly not the slimmest member of the class, but neither was I the most rotund. We spent a few minutes warming up with stretches and gentle bends. I felt the spandex in my leotard pulling me back into my original upright position after every bend. This was going to be okay, I could tell. And then the music started; and my friend, the aerobics instructor, became possessed!

She had us dancing and prancing and pivoting around in circles while some crazed maniac with a rock band shouted about "shakin' it, shakin' it, shakin' it." We were supposed to "grapevine left and take it to the corners," but I must have gotten my grapevine tangled up because I ran into someone and veered off toward the mirrors with a frightening speed. By the time I regained control, the class was facing the opposite direction doing something that looked like the Charleston. Just as I figured out the steps, the instructor yelled for everyone to "pony"; and they started bouncing and flailing their arms. I followed along as best I could, but my sweatband kept slipping down over my eyes; and I was gasping so loudly, I couldn't catch all the instructions.

When the music finally stopped, I staggered toward the water fountain on trembling legs.

"You're doing great!" my friend shouted across the room, waving at me.

I think I waved back. I don't remember. Right then I wanted to walk out and never go back; but I had no way to get home, so I stayed.

During the last ten minutes of the class, I really enjoyed myself. We stretched out on the floor on mats and relaxed to beautiful piano music. We envisioned peaceful pools and rippling streams and contracted and extended our muscles slowly. I wondered if I could just skip the first part of class and come for the "cool down."

When I asked my friend about that, she laughed. She thought I was kidding. I stuck with aerobics for a few weeks; but in the end, I folded up my pink leotard and put it in the box with the kids' Halloween costumes.

My aerobics instructor is still a friend, but she has moved on to seek other, more willing converts. In the meantime, I have become acquainted with a fascinating young woman who wants to teach me how to kayak.

Pamela Kennedy is a freelance writer of short stories, articles, essays, and children's books. Wife of a naval officer and mother of three children, she has made her home on both U.S. coasts and currently resides in Honolulu, Hawaii. She draws her material from her own experiences and memories, adding highlights from her imagination to enhance the story.

Anticipation

Carice Williams

The teacups are out of the cupboard,
And the table is set up for tea.
The hearth fire is glowing so brightly;
The kettle is whistling for me.

The curtains are starched and are hanging
On the windows so shiny and bright;
The door is wide open to welcome
The soft yellow rays of sunlight.

I wait for the ring of the doorbell
To announce that my callers are here.
I'm waiting, so patiently waiting,
To renew old friendships so dear.

At last I hear footsteps approaching,
And I eagerly run to the door
To welcome the friends of my childhood
And cherish sweet mem'ries of yore.

"There are few hours in life more agreeable than the hour dedicated to the ceremony known as afternoon tea."

*—Henry James,
The Portrait of a Lady*

Strawberry

Lemon

Bergamot

Hibiscus

Chicory

Cranberry

Jasmine

Chamomile

Orange

Rose Hips

Ideals'
Family Recipes

Favorite Recipes from the Ideals Family of Readers

Editor's Note: Please send us your best-loved recipes! Mail a typed copy of the recipe along with your name, address, and phone number to Ideals magazine, ATTN: Recipes, P.O. Box 305300, Nashville, Tennessee 37230. We will pay $10 for each recipe used. Recipes cannot be returned.

MAPLE NUT COFFEE TWIST

In a small saucepan, heat ¾ cup milk and ¼ cup butter or margarine over low heat until very warm but not boiling. In a large bowl, combine heated mixture, 1 cup all-purpose flour, 3 tablespoons granulated sugar, ½ teaspoon salt, 1 package active dry yeast, 1 teaspoon maple flavoring, and 1 egg. With an electric mixer at medium speed, beat 2 minutes. With a wooden spoon, stir in an additional 2 cups flour to make a soft dough. On a floured surface, knead dough until smooth and elastic, about 2 minutes. Place in a greased bowl; cover. Let rise in a warm place until light and doubled in size, about 1 hour.

In a small bowl, combine ½ cup granulated sugar, ⅓ cup chopped pecans, 1 teaspoon cinnamon, and 1 teaspoon maple flavoring. Set aside. In a separate bowl, place ¼ cup butter or margarine, melted. Set aside.

Punch down dough; divide and shape into 3 balls. Press or roll one ball of dough to cover bottom of a greased, 12¼-inch, round pizza pan. Brush with ⅓ of the melted butter; sprinkle with about ⅓ of pecan mixture. Repeat layering twice, ending with pecan mixture. To shape, place a glass (about 2 inches in diameter) in center of dough. With scissors, cut from outside edge to the glass, forming 16 pie-shaped wedges. Twist each wedge 5 times. Remove glass. Let dough rise until doubled in size, about 45 minutes. Preheat oven to 375° F. Bake 15 to 20 minutes or until golden brown. Cool 5 minutes in pan; remove to plate.

In a small bowl, combine 1 cup powdered sugar, 2 tablespoons melted butter or margarine, 1 to 2 tablespoons milk or water, and ½ teaspoon maple flavoring. Blend until smooth. Drizzle over warm coffee twist. Makes 16 servings.

Jessica and Katie Manni
Atlasburg, Pennsylvania

Lavender

Hibiscus

Chicory

Bergamot

Lemon

Chamomile

Cranberry

Jasmine

Strawberry

Lemon

Mama's Crumb Coffee Cake

Preheat oven to 350° F. In a medium bowl, combine 2 cups all-purpose flour, 3 tablespoons baking powder, and a pinch of salt; set aside. In a large bowl, cream ½ cup butter or margarine, softened, with ½ cup granulated sugar until light and fluffy. Add 2 eggs; stir well. Add 1 cup milk and 1 teaspoon vanilla. Gradually add flour mixture. With an electric mixer at medium speed, beat 2 minutes. Spread batter evenly in a greased, 9-by-13-by-2-inch baking pan. Set aside.

In a large bowl, combine 1½ cups granulated sugar, 1½ cups all-purpose flour, 3 tablespoons cinnamon, and a pinch of salt. With a pastry blender, cut in ½ cup butter or margarine, softened, and 4 tablespoons shortening until mixture resembles coarse crumbs. Top batter with crumb mixture. Bake 40 minutes. Makes 1 large coffee cake.

Gale Emig
Maspeth, New York

Bergamot

Zucchini Bread

Preheat oven to 350° F. In a large bowl, sift together 1½ cups all-purpose flour, 1 teaspoon ground cinnamon, ½ teaspoon baking soda, ¼ teaspoon baking powder, ½ teaspoon ground nutmeg, and ½ teaspoon salt; set aside. In a large bowl, beat together 1 cup granulated sugar; 1 cup finely shredded, unpeeled zucchini; and 1 egg. Stir flour mixture into zucchini mixture. Gently fold in ½ cup chopped walnuts. Turn batter into a greased, 8-by-4-by-2-inch loaf pan. Bake 55 to 60 minutes or until a wooden pick inserted into center comes out clean. Cool in pan 10 minutes. Turn out on wire rack to cool completely. Makes 1 loaf.

Holly Herndon
Boston, Massachusetts

Chicory

Hibiscus

Lavender

Cranberry Coffee Cake

Preheat oven to 350° F. In a large bowl, cream 1 cup butter or margarine with 1 cup granulated sugar until light and fluffy. Add 2 eggs, one at a time, beating well after each addition. Stir in ½ teaspoon almond extract. Stir in 2 cups sifted, self-rising flour alternately with 1 cup sour cream. Pour batter into a greased, 9-by-13-by-2-inch baking pan. Spoon one 8-ounce can whole berry cranberry sauce evenly over batter. Sprinkle with ½ cup chopped almonds. Bake 35 to 40 minutes or until cake pulls slightly away from sides of pan. In a small bowl, combine 1 cup powdered sugar, ½ teaspoon vanilla, and 2 tablespoons milk; stir until smooth. Drizzle over warm cake. Makes 1 large coffee cake.

Nancy Grady Wilson
Kenansville, North Carolina

Rose Hips

Strawberry

Jasmine

Cranberry

Chamomile

Orange

Tea and Talk

Ellen Rebecca Fenn

Wedgwood teacups line my cupboard shelves,
Beauty in a highly treasured prize;
The gath'ring years bring each cup dearer to
The envious glances from collectors' eyes.

Guests who love a spot of lemon tea
Find conversation quickly, smoothly flows
Between the sips from homey, lip-warmed cups,
A secret only weathered china knows.

Antique beauty I shall always keep
Displayed on cupboards tiptop; for myself,
When time to pour a spot of tea arrives,
I choose the lip-warm cup on lower shelf.

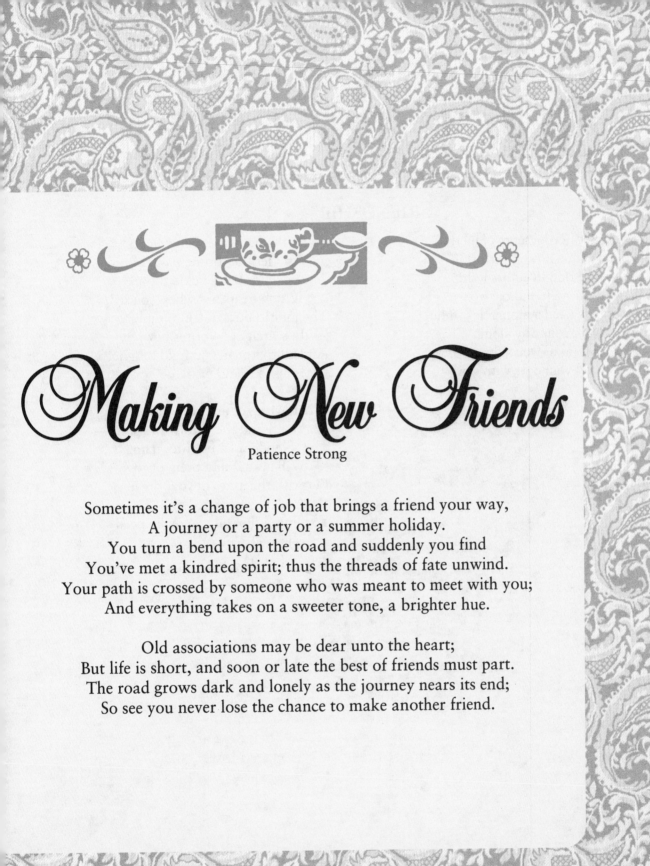

Making New Friends

Patience Strong

Sometimes it's a change of job that brings a friend your way,
A journey or a party or a summer holiday.
You turn a bend upon the road and suddenly you find
You've met a kindred spirit; thus the threads of fate unwind.
Your path is crossed by someone who was meant to meet with you;
And everything takes on a sweeter tone, a brighter hue.

Old associations may be dear unto the heart;
But life is short, and soon or late the best of friends must part.
The road grows dark and lonely as the journey nears its end;
So see you never lose the chance to make another friend.

A SLICE OF LIFE

Edgar A. Guest

FRIENDSHIP

You do not need a score of men
　　To laugh and sing with you;
You can be rich in comradeship
　　With just a friend or two.
You do not need a monarch's smile
　　To light your way along;
Through weal or woe a friend or two
　　Will fill your days with song.

So let the many go their way,
　　And let the throng pass by;
The crowd is but a fickle thing
　　Which hears not when you sigh.
The multitude is quick to run
　　In search of favorites new,
And all that man can hold for grief
　　Is just a friend or two.

When winds of failure start to blow,
　　You'll find the throng has gone—
The splendor of a brighter flame
　　Will always lure them on;
But with the ashes of your dreams,
　　And all you hoped to do,
You'll find that all you really need
　　Is just a friend or two.

You cannot know the multitude,
    However hard you try.
It cannot sit about your hearth;
    It cannot hear you sigh;
It cannot read the heart of you,
    Or know the hurts you bear;
Its cheers are all for happy men
    And not for those in care.

So let the throng go on its way,
    And let the crowd depart;
But one or two will keep the faith
    When you are sick at heart;
And rich you'll be, and comforted,
    When gray skies hide the blue
If you can turn and share your grief
    With just a friend or two.

Edgar A. Guest began his illustrious career in 1895 at the age of fourteen when his work first appeared in the Detroit Free Press. *His column was syndicated in over 300 newspapers, and he became known as "The Poet of the People."*

Patrick McRae is an artist who lives in the Milwaukee, Wisconsin, area. He has created nostalgic artwork for Ideals *for more than a decade, and his favorite models are his wife and three children.*

Beyond the Fog of Years

Hilda Butler Farr

If we should meet upon the street
Some unexpected day,
You'd take my hand;
And there we'd stand
Without a word to say.

And then, my dear,
Our hearts would clear;
And we would stroll along,
Forgetting years and bitter tears
In memories and song.

I'd see your smile a little while,
And clouds would slip away
If we could meet upon the street
Some unexpected day.

OUR HERITAGE

FROM *THE REMINISCENCES OF CARL SCHURZ*

Carl Schurz

I remember vividly the feelings which almost oppressed me as I first sat down in my chair in the Senate chamber. Now I had actually reached the most exalted public position to which my boldest dreams of ambition had hardly dared to aspire. I was still a young man, just forty. Little more than sixteen years had elapsed since I had landed on these shores, a homeless waif saved from the wreck of a revolutionary movement in Europe. Then I was enfolded in the generous hospitality of the American people opening to me, as freely as to its own children, the great opportunities of the new world. And here I was now, a member of the highest law-making body of the greatest of republics. Should I ever be able fully to pay my debt of gratitude to this country, and to justify the honors that had been heaped upon me? To accomplish this, my conception of duty could not be pitched too high. I recorded a vow in my own heart that I would at least honestly endeavor to fulfill that duty; that I would conscientiously adhere to the principle *salus populi suprema lex* [the welfare of the people is the highest law]; that I would never be a sycophant of power nor a flatterer of the multitude; that, if need be, I would stand up alone for my conviction of truth and right; and that there would be no personal sacrifice too great for my devotion to the Republic.

ABOUT THE AUTHOR

Carl Schurz was perhaps one of our most famous naturalized citizens. After participating in a failed revolution in Prussia in 1852, he fled his homeland at age twenty-three. Living first in Switzerland, then England, Schurz found his way to the United States. Looking back, he said, "The fatherland [Prussia] was closed to me. England was to me a foreign country, and would always remain so. Where, then? 'To America,' I said to myself. . . . "

Schurz first migrated to the German community of Philadelphia, later to Wisconsin, where he was a leader in the antislavery movement and campaigned for Abraham Lincoln. In his fifty-four years of American life, Schurz was a practicing lawyer, U.S. senator, minister to Spain under President Lincoln, Major General in the Civil War, Secretary of the Interior under President Hayes, editor of the New York *Evening Post*, editor of a German-language newspaper, and chief editorial writer for *Harper's Weekly*. Schurz became a prodigious writer later in life and filled more than sixteen volumes. He died in 1906, leaving a legacy of writings unsurpassed in their patriotic fervor.

Weekend Guest

Mary Elizabeth Raymond

I'm Grandma to a girl in green,
  My special weekend guest,
The proudest scout I've ever seen
  With badges on her vest.

With summer camp and winter snow,
  She loves all scouting fun.
She takes me back to long ago
  When I was such a one.

We took a hike around the block
  Collecting nuts and leaves.
We learned to sew a pretty frock,
  Then played till it was eve,

Sang silly songs, consumed "s'mores";
  She won a pillow fight.
We dragged our sleeping bags outdoors
  And giggled half the night.

She whispered tricks and pranks to play,
  The kind I tried back then;
Some fifty years just trooped away,
  And I'm a kid again.

LISA C. RAGAN

JULIETTE "DAISY" GORDON LOW

Despite early warnings from male leaders of turning girls into tomboys, Juliette Gordon Low rallied women throughout the United States to join her in an effort to bolster self-esteem, instill patriotism, and develop an appreciation for practical skills in the young girls of America. Establishing a firm foundation for her organization was hard work; but after relentless perseverance, her dream became reality when she founded the Girl Scouts of America.

Born in 1860 in Savannah, Georgia, to socially prominent, wealthy parents, Juliette Gordon Low showed a strong, independent spirit at an early age. At age eight, she saved a young child from drowning, an uncommon feat for one so young. Nicknamed Daisy by her family, she displayed a charming wit and considerable artistic talent, which were traits she shared with her mother. She was, however, closer to her father, a Confederate war hero, from whom she often sought advice and comfort.

Educated at private schools, Daisy demonstrated a particular affinity for the arts, a talent she would enjoy the rest of her life. At school in New York City, she studied painting, wrote plays, and performed in amateur theatre productions. As part of her continued education, Daisy traveled throughout the eastern United States and Europe in her early twenties. After a nine-year marriage to William Mackay Low, the wealthy son of a Savannah family, Daisy found herself widowed and growing increasingly deaf from an ill-treated earache.

In 1911, Daisy formed a close friendship with someone who would remain a dear friend the rest of her life—General Sir Robert Baden-Powell, the founder of the Boy Scouts in England. From Sir Robert, Daisy learned of the Girl Guides, England's female counterpart to the Boy Scouts; and her enthusiasm was piqued immediately. She liked the idea of teaching young girls useful, practical skills that were unlike the lessons she learned in finishing school. Back in the United States the next year, Daisy told a friend, "I've got something for Savannah, and all America, and all the world; and we're going to start it tonight."

Daisy organized the first troops in Savannah, where they enjoyed considerable popularity. With Daisy as their leader, the girls took camping trips, sewed their own uniforms, and learned first aid skills. She sought to instill in each girl a strong sense of pride in herself. While she loved working directly with the girls, Daisy knew her true calling was to set up troops across the country. In 1913, she traveled to Washington, D.C., to set up a national organization. At first, many of the top men of the Boy Scouts of America opposed Daisy's venture, mostly because of the use of the word *scouts* in conjunction with girls. The Boy Scouts launched letter-writing campaigns to articulate their dissent and even threatened to sue over use of the word. Daisy literally and figuratively turned a deaf ear to their complaints. Finally, in 1915, the Girl Scouts of America was born.

As president of the newly formed Girl Scouts, Daisy Low completely dedicated herself to her work. Financially she made many personal donations to her cause and funded a significant part of the program's needs in its infancy. Most importantly, though, Daisy traveled throughout the country to rally women and girls to her cause; and, thanks to her charm and determination, she inspired many women to become leaders and form troops in their hometowns. The vision Daisy held for America's young girls can be summed up in the Girl Scout promise: "On my honor I will try to do my duty to God and my country, to help other people at all times, to obey the Girl Scout laws." Daisy sought to instill in the girls a respect for independence which she cherished in herself. In the first Girl Scout handbook, entitled *How Girls Can Help Their Country*, girls were encouraged to consider becoming doctors or aviators, but cautioned not to act like boys, for "it is better to be a real girl such as no boy can possibly be."

Although she resigned as president in 1920, Daisy Low continued to work at a national and international level as the founder of the Girl Scouts until her death in 1926 from cancer. Before her death, she organized the first international conference at the new Girl Scout camp in New York; it was her last important achievement. She was buried in her Girl Scout uniform in Savannah, with a telegram from the Girl Scout president in her pocket which read: "You are not only the first Girl Scout, you are the best Girl Scout of them all."

A woman of remarkable determination, Daisy Low pursued her dream of establishing a successful scouting organization for girls not only in the United States, but also throughout the world. Often described as possessing an eternal youthfulness, Daisy put her outspoken, independent spirit, as well as her social position, to use by sparking enthusiasm for the Girl Scouts wherever she went. Thanks to Daisy Low, millions of bright, independent young girls today are proud to call themselves members of the Girl Scouts of America.

ENLARGEMENT

June Masters Bacher

I pitched my tent, designed for one,
And stood aside; my work was done.

It looked so small, though well prepared—
A something built, but nothing shared.

"Enlarge your tent; stretch out your twine,"
Called out this yearning heart of mine.

And so I stretched the stakes out wide;
And friendship came and dwelt inside.

Make new friends,
But keep the old.
One is silver;
The other, gold.

—traditional camp song,
to be sung in a round

Remember When

THE BRIDGE
Lisa C. Ragan

Many years ago, I was proud to be a beanie-wearing Brownie scout, and I applied myself most earnestly to merit as many badges as I could. Once my tenure as a Brownie ended and I had finally earned my "wings" in order to "fly up" to the Girl Scouts, I had acquired many handy skills and made many good friends. The most important thing I gained, however, did not result in a colorful badge to be sewn onto my brown uniform; it was something I found in myself.

It happened during the summer of my seventh year when I spent one whole character-molding week at Brownie day camp. Since the closest my family ever came to camping was roasting marshmallows over the charcoal grill in the back-yard, I was thrilled to "rough it" in the wilderness with other brave scouts. We spent the first day of camp contentedly organizing our campsite, collecting wild-flowers, and weaving baskets. The rest of the week progressed happily swim-ming, hiking, and making crafts. On the last day, however, our troop leaders announced that we were going on a morning hike to Farmer's Meadow; and to get there, we'd have to cross *the monkey bridge.*

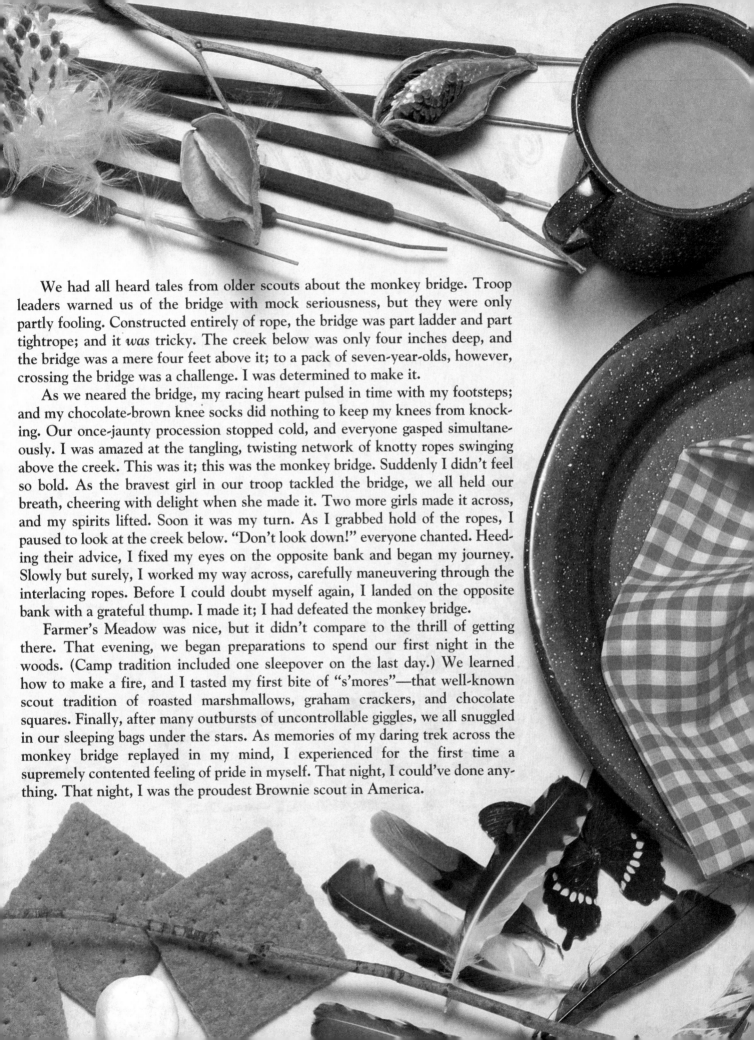

We had all heard tales from older scouts about the monkey bridge. Troop leaders warned us of the bridge with mock seriousness, but they were only partly fooling. Constructed entirely of rope, the bridge was part ladder and part tightrope; and it *was* tricky. The creek below was only four inches deep, and the bridge was a mere four feet above it; to a pack of seven-year-olds, however, crossing the bridge was a challenge. I was determined to make it.

As we neared the bridge, my racing heart pulsed in time with my footsteps; and my chocolate-brown knee socks did nothing to keep my knees from knocking. Our once-jaunty procession stopped cold, and everyone gasped simultaneously. I was amazed at the tangling, twisting network of knotty ropes swinging above the creek. This was it; this was the monkey bridge. Suddenly I didn't feel so bold. As the bravest girl in our troop tackled the bridge, we all held our breath, cheering with delight when she made it. Two more girls made it across, and my spirits lifted. Soon it was my turn. As I grabbed hold of the ropes, I paused to look at the creek below. "Don't look down!" everyone chanted. Heeding their advice, I fixed my eyes on the opposite bank and began my journey. Slowly but surely, I worked my way across, carefully maneuvering through the interlacing ropes. Before I could doubt myself again, I landed on the opposite bank with a grateful thump. I made it; I had defeated the monkey bridge.

Farmer's Meadow was nice, but it didn't compare to the thrill of getting there. That evening, we began preparations to spend our first night in the woods. (Camp tradition included one sleepover on the last day.) We learned how to make a fire, and I tasted my first bite of "s'mores"—that well-known scout tradition of roasted marshmallows, graham crackers, and chocolate squares. Finally, after many outbursts of uncontrollable giggles, we all snuggled in our sleeping bags under the stars. As memories of my daring trek across the monkey bridge replayed in my mind, I experienced for the first time a supremely contented feeling of pride in myself. That night, I could've done anything. That night, I was the proudest Brownie scout in America.

Friendliness

Leisetta Brodt

I love the friendly way you speak.
   There's something in your voice
That seems so fascinating, sweet;
   It is my fondest choice.

For when you speak, I feel so near.
   Somehow you have a way
Of speaking words so full of cheer;
   It brightens my whole day.

It seems as though the way you speak
   Is just a part of you.
You speak the same to all you meet;
   You're just as friendly too.

And as you go along your way,
   You play friendship's fond part
To brighten all the bleakest days
   With warmth from your own heart.

Bless Everyone

Marlene Erwin

This morning when I wakened
And saw the sun above,
I softly said, "Good morning, Lord,
Bless everyone I love."

Right away I thought of you
And said a loving prayer
That He would bless you specially
And keep you free from care.

I thought of all the happiness
A day could hold in store;
I wished it all for you because
No one deserves it more.

I felt so warm and good inside;
My heart was all aglow.
I heard God say He heard my prayer;
He hears them all, you know.

FOR THE CHILDREN

ARTWORK BY RUSS FLINT

THE ARROW AND THE SONG

Henry Wadsworth Longfellow

I shot an arrow into the air,
It fell to earth, I knew not where;
For, so swiftly it flew, the sight
Could not follow it in its flight.

I breathed a song into the air,
It fell to earth, I knew not where;
For who has sight so keen and strong,
That it can follow the flight of song?

Long, long afterward, in an oak
I found the arrow, still unbroke;
And the song, from beginning to end,
I found again in the heart of a friend.

The unique perspective of Russ Flint's artistic style has made him a favorite of Ideals *readers for many years. A resident of California and father of four, Russ Flint has illustrated a children's Bible and many other books.*

Friendship

Carice Williams

In truest form, a friendship rare
   Is hard to e'er define;
For it's composed of many things
   In intricate design.

It is a star that lights the way
   When darkness hovers near;
It is the warmth of hearth fires bright
   That always seem to cheer.

It is a lovely melody
   Grown sweeter with the years
That has a way of bringing joy,
   Dispelling cares and fears.

Its meaning only can be felt
   Instead of e'er expressed;
But well we know that friendship true
   Brings joy to every breast.

BITS & PIECES

The comfort of having a friend may be taken away,
but not that of having had one.

—*Seneca*

Without wearing any mask we are conscious of,
we have a special face for each friend.

—*Oliver Wendell Holmes*

Friendship is a serious affection, the most sublime
of all affections, because it is founded on principle
and cemented by time.

—*Mary Wollstonecraft*

A friend is one who knows you as you are,
understands where you've been,
accepts who you've become,
and still gently invites you to grow.

—*Author Unknown*

Scatter thus your seeds of kindness
All enriching as you go.
Leave them. Trust the Harvest Giver;
He will make each seed to grow.
So until the happy end
Your life shall never lack a friend.

—*Author Unknown*

It takes a long time to grow an old friend.

—*John Leonard*

*I*nstead of a gem, or even a flower, we should cast
the gift of a loving thought into the heart of a
friend—that would be giving as the angels give.
—George MacDonald

A friend is one who knows all about you and
likes you just the same.
—Elbert Green Hubbard

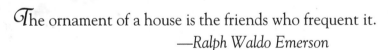

*T*he ornament of a house is the friends who frequent it.
—Ralph Waldo Emerson

*B*lessed are they who have the gift of making friends,
for it is one of God's best gifts. It involves many things,
but above all, the power of going out of one's self and
appreciating whatever is noble and loving in another.
—Thomas Hughes

"*W*hat is the secret of your life?" asked Mrs. Browning,
the poet, of Charles Kingsley, the novelist.
"Tell me, that I may make mine beautiful too."
He replied, "I had a friend."
—related by William Channing Gannett

Bonds of Friendship

Hilda Butler Farr

When days are filled with sunshine,
How close we hold a friend;
It's good to share the laughter,
The dreams that have no end.
And it is fun exchanging
Some episode of fun
And finding much in common
In all that you have done.

But when the days are shadowed,
Perhaps with pain or grief,
The bonds of friendship tighten
Almost beyond belief.
And burdens aren't so heavy
When someone takes your hand;
And not a word is needed
To prove she understands.

The world would be so lonely
In sunny hours or gray
Without the gift of friendship
To help us every day.

HANDMADE HEIRLOOM

HANDMADE STATIONERY. Created by Mary Skarmeas. Jerry Koser Photography.

HANDMADE PAPER

Mary Skarmeas

Ialways look forward to the days when I open the mailbox to find a letter from my dearest childhood friend, Emily. For years, Emily and I shared all the joys and trials of growing up; after we were both married, she moved far away from our small hometown, and her letters provided a cherished link to a much-missed companion. Not only were Emily's letters heartwarming, but they were beautiful as well, due to the colorful handmade paper on which her kind words were written. Each

piece was speckled with myriad bits of pinks, blues, and greens. Knowing the care she had taken in making the colorful, one-of-a-kind paper made her letters all the more special.

Papermaking itself is an ancient craft with origins in second century China. The scribe Ts'ai Lun is credited with the first modern paper, for he discovered the process of creating paper out of macerated wood pulp. Before Ts'ai Lun's time, the Chinese scribes produced their religious and sacred texts on wood, bamboo, or cloth. Similar ancient media were used by the Europeans until they began making paper in the twelfth century. In 1690, the first American paper mill began operating near Philadelphia, making paper by using methods not too far removed from those of the early Chinese.

Modern technology has made mass machine production of paper possible and has given us the plentiful paper of uniform color and texture that gives pages to our books, fills our mailboxes, stacks high on our desks, and, more often than not, winds up in the recycling pile or the wastebasket. But the basic principles used in mass production are little changed from those that guided the Chinese centuries ago; paper is still made from dried and pressed pulp, most often wood pulp. With a little research and a few basic tools, today's craftsperson can rediscover the old methods of papermaking and create extraordinary sheets of handmade paper truly worth holding on to.

The craft of papermaking is enjoying a revival, and instructive articles and books for the beginner are easy to find. Do a bit of research, but don't be hesitant to plunge in; this is truly a learn-by-doing craft. Handmade paper, like mass-produced paper, is made from pulp. Whereas many mills rely on trees for their pulp, the individual can rely on previously used paper as the foundation of the pulp. Any color or texture will do, as long as it is absorbent. Tear the paper into small strips and pieces, soak in water for several hours, and then macerate in an electric blender until it is a thick liquid. Pour the pulp over a mesh screen in a wooden frame. The object is to coat the screen with an even, flat layer of pulp. This residue, when dried, becomes paper.

These days, handmade paper is everywhere. I have discovered lovely personal journals and greeting cards made with beautiful, rich-textured handmade paper. These exquisite items might lead one to believe that papermaking is a craft only for the sophisticated, trained craftsperson; but, as I learned, this is a great craft for beginners. It may take hours of practice and an artistic flair to make the handmade paper that ends up as a greeting card or a diary, but on my first try I produced a sheet of true paper—somewhat lumpy, yes, but a beautiful, delicate sheet of paper nonetheless. I was hooked.

Making paper is a rewarding craft; and once you begin, you won't want to stop. "One more sheet," I found myself uttering over and over again as I learned how to make the pulp just the right consistency and the perfect thickness on the sieve. Part of the fun is experimenting with all the materials that can be used to create your unique paper—a true testimony to the art of recycling. Bits of herbs, pine needles, flower petals, leaves, moss, silk thread, satin ribbon, decorative napkins, food coloring, coffee, tea, pages from a discarded book, even that most abundant of resources, junk mail, can be added to the basic pulp for color and texture. If you can cut it up into small pieces, you can add it to your pulp. Only the fully dried sheet will reveal the results.

Papermaking is not the craft typically learned at your mother's knee; yet it is a craft perfectly suited to our age. It takes nothing from our precious natural resources, and it creates something beautiful out of discarded items. Handmade paper can become a greeting card for a special occasion. Adorned with a photograph, it can become a birth announcement; with calligraphy, you can create wedding invitations. The truly ambitious can create notecards with matching envelopes—no two will be alike—for their most treasured correspondents.

Handmade paper lends a special grace, style, and permanence to the written word, as attested by dozens of Emily's colorful letters that I have saved through the years. The constant correspondence between Emily and me has kept us faithful friends, and her notes are still often written on her beautiful handmade paper. With my newfound skill at papermaking, I've decided to return the favor; my next letter to her will be written on lavender-flecked, handmade stationery—the perfect medium to let her know how much her friendship has brightened my life.

Mary Skarmeas lives in Danvers, Massachusetts, and has recently earned her bachelor's degree in English at Suffolk University. Mother of four and grandmother of two, Mary loves all crafts, especially knitting.

Friend

Craig E. Sathoff

Dear Friend,

It seems that it is hard to say
That which I deeply feel,
To thank you for your gifts to me
Of help and trust and zeal.

Your faith in me that I'd succeed
When I felt down and blue
Proved just the boost I seemed to need
To see my problems through.

You cheered me in the troubling times
With your lighthearted smile,
And yet your steady hand was there
To lend support the while.

Although the miles have come between,
And you're not here today,
I'd like to send my special thanks.
And then I'd like to say

That as you face each daily task,
One thing is surely true:
My thoughts and prayers and memories
Are there today with you.

Your Friend

Talking to Amber

Gladys Taber

A kitten brings a special magic to a house, but it cannot compare with a mature relationship. And since Amber and I live alone, we have had ample time to explore our own personalities and reach a high level of understanding. I have never been able to talk to myself for comfort. Although I am a verbal person, I do not find the furniture or even my beloved house itself a satisfying audience. I need an active listener, and Amber is a listening cat. Unlike people, she never interrupts. She never criticizes me for what I say. But her speaking tail responds when my voice is deep with sadness. Her ears stand like small sails when I am excited. And when I am in a philosophical mood and speak thoughtfully, she turns that wedge-shaped head toward me, and the wisdom of past ages seems to be in her eyes. Then when I fall silent she resumes scrubbing her immaculate face.

Amber reflects my mood instantly. For instance, she is not a football addict, but when a game is tied 24-24 and one field goal will determine the winner, she leaps into my lap and her whiskers quiver at my excitement. And at such moments she does not tell me she wants another dish of minced beef.

If I am despondent, the look of anxiety on her face makes me pull myself together. And when my thoughts are racing like wind-blown clouds, I can always depend on Amber to listen. In fact, she is a better listener than some of my friends, who really do not pay any attention when I want to discuss how many shades of gray there are in the sky and how many on the land on a cloudy January afternoon.

Amber pays considered attention to whatever I say. Her answers may be a shake of the lissome tail, or a quiver of the golden-silver whiskers, or a spreading of beautiful paws, or at times a polite yawn that speaks plainly, saying it is one o'clock in the morning and it is bedtime, even for us night people!

But if I have trouble sleeping and get up at two or three, she wakes instantly, ready to listen again to any kind of nonsense I may have dreamed up.

She purrs!

Yesterday I discovered that a new neighbor had come to call. Afterward she telephoned. "I wanted to ask you about a trashman, but I knew you had company and didn't want to disturb you."

"I didn't have any company all day," I said.

"Well, I thought it was odd because there was no car in your yard, but I heard you having a conversation with someone."

"Oh, that," I said. "I was just talking to Amber."

"I guess she must have walked up from the beach. I haven't met her."

"Do come again," I said. "Amber is my Abyssinian cat."

There was a silence. I knew what she was thinking. Writers are supposed to be odd, but whoever thought they might hold conversations with a cat?

When I told this to Amber, her tail rotated, her ears flicked, and she began pawing on the pages of my book. Her message was definite. "Forget about new neighbors. Why don't you stop digging into that stupid book and talk to me?"

"Cats are supposed to be independent," I said. For answer she flipped a page with a long delicate arm, thus losing my place in a very thick book.

Over our snack of sliced red apples spread with cream cheese, I explained that humans have a great many conventions. Singing in the shower is acceptable. So is singing along with records, even if one cannot carry a tune. But walking around doing housework while chattering away to oneself raises the eyebrows of any neighbors who happen to overhear.

"Amber," I said, "I am an eccentric. My favorite teenage protégé told me that once when I was describing the meanings of various colors. And I guess it's true."

In the years that we have been together, Amber and I have had many conversations on many subjects. No matter whether she is busy sharpening her claws on the forbidden green armchair or pushing a velvet nose in the spaghetti sauce, she will always stop and listen when I have some thought to share. And she will let me know how she herself feels. I have jotted down most of these conversations because they express the experiences we have shared. Happiness and sorrow have walked through our door; laughter and tears have companioned us. Amber has grown up, and I presumably have grown wiser. But we have walked together and found something new in every day to be grateful for.

Tribute to a Friend

Alton J. Chapman

I never come to you, dear friend,
   And walk away without
Some new enrichment in my heart
   That does away with doubt.
I always find more courage on
   The days I have great need;
For when I come to you, I go
   So comforted indeed.

I've searched my mind for words and find
   No words that really tell
How much your friendship means to me,
   Your love and care as well.
If I could find one shining word
   So you would somehow know,
But this is where I'm bound to fail;
   My heart tells me it's so.

There is no word or phrase for one
   On whom I so depend
Except these words right from my heart:
   "God bless you," precious friend.

CORNER

INKWELLS

by Lara Davies

My mother has always been an avid collector of antiques and old treasures tried and true. When I was a child, she would pile the entire family in the car and take us what she referred to as "antiquing." We spent many delightful Saturdays together exploring flea markets and antique shops and chatting with the proprietors, who often shared marvelous tales about their own collections and how they acquired their favorite pieces.

While vacationing in New England one summer, my family came across a store in Nantucket whose front window was filled with an eclectic collection of inkwells, from simple colored-glass bottles to ornate china figurines that nearly hid the well among a flurry of porcelain flowers. Once inside the shop, we met the owner, Mr. Sudbury, who was clearly knowledgeable about his wares. He served tea to my sister and me as he zealously explained the intriguing history behind these small wells and the significant role they once played in communication and education. When asked about the startling variety of inkwells he offered, Mr. Sudbury explained that ink was kept close at hand, and the inkwells that held it were designed to fit various tastes, decors, and writing situations. Thus his collection ranged from a tiny travelers' well used for en route correspondence to a fancy gold and silver one that I was sure once graced the desk of an elegant room.

Perhaps the simplest inkwells in the quaint shop's display were the small glass ones once used in olden-day schoolhouses. My sister and I listened intently as Mr. Sudbury described how each week the teacher would select one responsible boy, who would strut proudly to the supply cabinet to find the large container of ink with a clear tube attached. As he walked down each row, he would stop at every desk and cautiously fill each child's inkwell with that week's allotment of ink.

My mother was quick to notice how enthralled I was by Mr. Sudbury's stories. Before we left the shop, she bought me a green, patterned-glass inkwell, which became the first piece of my collection; I was hooked. In the years to follow, I added dozens of inkwells to my display, from a cast-iron figurine shaped like the head of a wide-eyed owl to a cut-crystal cube in the most brilliant shade of blue. Each inkwell is unique and adds its own beauty, flair, or whimsy to my collection.

I discovered my best find on a trip to a local antique mall with Mother, who is thrilled that I now share her fervor for searching out old treasures. While she was busy examining the handles on a lovely mahogany desk, I was immediately drawn to the desk's surface and a hand-carved, wooden inkwell shaped like a nut. The nut, which opens to reveal the well, rests on a large carved leaf, whose edges curl up to hold an idle pen.

I was so inspired by my interesting new piece that I tried using it as it was originally intended. I eagerly purchased a bottle of ink and a quill pen, forgetting the fact that I am quite unfamiliar with the subtleties of pen and ink penmanship. After several attempts that resulted in illegible blobs, I passed the bottle of ink on to a calligrapher friend; but I had gained a newfound respect for my collectibles and the patience and skill of their original owners.

My collection now serves decorative purposes only, and my eagerness is limited to finding new pieces and learning about their past. Perhaps I'll uncover the next prized addition to my collection this weekend; Mom and I are making yet another excursion to search for once-loved antiques, and we're both keeping an eye out for an old, wooden school desk, the perfect "home" for my favorite inkwells.

ANTIQUE INKSTAND AND INKWELL. Jessie Walker Associates.

A Drop of Information

If you would like to start an inkwell collection of your own, here are some facts you will want to know:

History

- Made of horn or leather during the Middle Ages and called inkhorns or inkpots
- Commissioned in gold or silver by royalty
- In high demand during the 19th and 20th centuries as emphasis on education and business flourished
- Produced by well-known companies worldwide such as Longway in France, Coalport in England, and dozens of American companies. Makers seldom left identifying marks.
- Reflected styles of specific periods such as Rococo, Victorian, and Art Nouveau
- Replaced by ballpoint pens in the 1950s

Common Styles

- Inkwells shaped as birds, clowns, shoes, cottages, snails, camels, and other animals
- Hand-painted floral or scenic designs
- Cone-shaped styles with weighted bottoms designed to sit on a desk
- Fancy Victorian styles featuring gaudy, gilded designs and human figurines
- Matching covers, stoppers, or hinged lids to keep ink from drying
- Matching inkstands, blotters, or pen rests

Frequent Materials

- Gold or silver
- Hand-painted porcelain
- Patterned, pressed, or colored glass
- Hand-blown and colored crystal
- Glazed pottery or stoneware
- French faience (a type of fine pottery)
- Ornate, polished brass and copper
- Cast iron or pewter
- Carved wood
- Polished stone or marble
- Plastic or Bakelite

Interesting Pieces

- Small, rare travelers' inkwells, often resembling pillboxes
- Souvenir inkwells from the early twentieth century depicting such attractions as the Eiffel Tower or Mount Vernon
- Japanese teakettle designs that hold the ink in the round "kettle" and the quill or pen in the "spout"
- A Wedgwood inkwell made of jasperware and shaped like Aladdin's lamp
- Papier-mâché wells from China and Japan, glazed in shiny black enamels and hand-painted with flowers

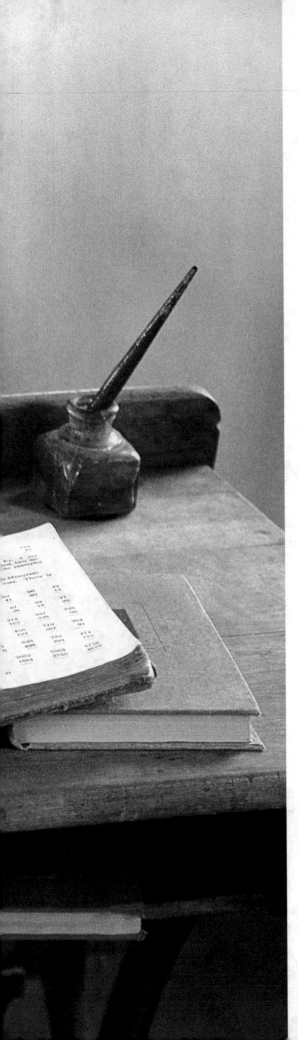

School Days, Country Style

Craig E. Sathoff

The years I spent in country school
    Were special years for me
Of mental growth and social skill
    And splendid harmony.

The spelling bees and penmanship,
    The recitation bench,
Then plays to act and games to share
    When we would break for lunch.

Some nights I lingered after school
    To help my teacher fill
The inkwells in the students' desks,
    So careful not to spill.

And though my teacher could be strict,
    She always was a friend;
And thus I loved to help her there
    When long school days would end.

And oh, the fun of walking home
    Through fields of ripened grain,
Collecting buckeyes—heaps of them—
    For bonfire time again.

For buckeyes thrown into a fire
    Made quite a hearty pop!
As fireworks of yesteryear,
    I found them hard to top.

The years in country school were filled
    With knowledge and good will.
They've been a strength down through the years;
    They linger with me still.

Devotions

Pamela Kennedy

Faithful are the wounds of a friend;
but the kisses of an enemy are deceitful.

–Proverbs 27:6

FAITHFUL FRIENDS

I pulled the bundle of mail from the mailbox with anticipation, wondering what surprises were hidden in it today. Perhaps I would win a million dollars, receive a letter from family, or find a party invitation along with the inevitable bills and catalogues.

A small, blue envelope slipped from the stack and fluttered to the ground. Picking it up, I recognized the return address of a dear friend with whom I had enjoyed lunch earlier in the week. Once inside, I settled at the kitchen table to read the note. She cheerfully recalled our terrific lunch and conversation, but then her tone changed to one of concern as she reminded me of the time we had spent discussing a mutual acquaintance—gossiping, really. She closed the note with this statement: "After thinking about what I said to you, I feel I should apologize to you and Maryanne. I wasn't a very good friend to either of you."

Her remark startled me. It made me think about what it means to be a faithful friend. Most would agree that being a friend implies being loyal when we are face to face, as well as when our backs our turned. But my friend had grasped a deeper truth: faithful friendship also means holding one another accountable when we sense danger on the horizon of our relationship. How easy it is today to isolate ourselves from one another, to avoid confrontation, to keep our friendships on a superficial level and thus deprive each other of opportunities for growth and maturity. It was not easy for my friend to declare her feelings of failure to me, but she risked that in order to deepen the honesty of our relationship. What I appreciated as much, however, was the gentle reminder that I too had wandered into the dangerous trap of gossip.

In the book of Proverbs, King Solomon writes, "Faithful are the wounds of a friend; but the kisses of an enemy are deceitful." When friends are truly faithful, they tell us not only what we want to hear, but also what we need to hear. This friendly honesty strengthens and encourages healthy, growing relationships.

Prayer: Dear Father, grant me the humility to receive honest correction and the grace to be a faithful friend.

THE TEA PARTY
August Haerning, Artist
Superstock

MAPLE LEAVES WITH FROST. Monroe, Oregon. Dennis Frates/Oregon Scenics.

First Frost

Grace E. Easley

The frost-gowns of the willows,
In white, pulled-thread designs,
Drape lightly through the dawning
And cling to slender lines.
Rising through the silence,
The swirl of gray mist makes
Patterns of weightless shadows
Above the placid lakes.

78

FROSTED MAPLE LEAVES. Superstock.

Clustered on onyx branches,
Their faces to the breeze,
The leaves of beaded crystal
Adorn the stately trees.
And yards of coral ribbon,
All streaked with mauve and gold,
Blend through silken skies almost
Too lovely to behold.

Over the fence and thicket,
The spider webs of dew,
Along the narrow footpaths,
The glitter of a new
And iridescent splendor
Lies thickly everywhere.
What need have I for further proof
To know that God is here?

My Favorite Autumn Memory

Personal Stories of Treasured Memories from the Ideals Family of Readers

The Homestead

The thirty maples, dressed in an array of brilliant oranges, vibrant reds, and clear yellows, stood like a color guard along the narrow country lane leading to the old homestead. They had stood there since the early 1800s, faithfully bearing the forceful winds, the heavy, sticky snows, and the destructive storms that took a toll on their swinging branches and strong vitality.

Standing straight and tall, they had proffered a quiet welcome to each guest journeying down the dirt driveway. To the casual stroller they offered refreshing shade in which confidential conversation and relaxation could be enjoyed. They beckoned to the noisy, adventurous children to climb into their spreading branches. In the quiet of early spring, they gave their strength and nourishment to supply sap for the much-coveted syrup. The age-old sentinels had been more than mere onlookers at life; they had been participants.

On either side of the lane were acres of cornfields which at the fall season had undergone the heavy, killing frosts. The stalks stood in their long, brown robes waving their arms in the breeze and inviting the blue jay with his top hat to feast on the kernels. The crow, with a laugh, needed no invitation to sweep down and steal a nourishing bite.

Many times I had walked the bumpy road, kicking at a pebble and stopping to pick a plump bunch of succulent purple grapes to enjoy the smooth texture and sweet flavor. As a child I had hidden behind the rough trunks of the maples where I thought I could hide from God when I had been naughty.

The driveway led to a large, slate-roofed, plainly built farmhouse with its adjoining red barns and pastures of contented cows. Hand-picked stones of all sizes and shapes had been carefully laid to make a four-foot-high, gray wall outlining the lawns that surrounded the house. Dense green shrubbery and brightly colored mums adorned the perimeter of the stone structure.

One bright autumn day I drove to the old homestead. The stately trees had grown old and feeble, a few succumbing to nature. I sat immersed in a flood of remembrances that swept over me like an ocean at high tide. I tried to quiet my inner reactions; but being unsuccessful, I gave my mind free rein.

I recalled the times that I had raced back and forth on the stone walls, shouting, screaming, singing, laughing, feeling as free as a bird soaring on the wind. I had heard my mother call to me from the kitchen, and with the same exuberance I had run onto the porch giving the screen door a slam as I slowed my pace. A strong molasses aroma had filled the air.

My heart filled with gladness in recalling a happy childhood with loving, God-fearing parents; and my mouth watered as I remembered the thick, chewy, fresh-from-the-oven molasses cookies that were always waiting for me.

Dorothy Schweinforth
Scotia, New York

Indian Summer

Growing up in the Midwest gave me a deep appreciation for the four seasons. The cooler days of autumn were always welcome after the hot days of summer, but often seemed to get a little too cool just a little too fast. Sometimes, along about mid-October, we would be blessed with a few days of glorious, warm weather. Those days of Indian Summer always felt like a special gift, and the colors of the fall season seemed especially intensified.

My family would often take advantage of those precious days by traveling to a neighboring county for a covered bridge festival. This was a special treat since it meant caramel apples and hay rides and sing-alongs. Thus, Indian Summer came to mean for me an opportunity to celebrate the beautiful autumn weather with the special people in my life.

Chesnye Clark
Oklahoma City, Oklahoma

Autumn Sketch

Another summer is gone. Autumn is here. Even if the calendar hangs unused on the wall, signs of autumn are everywhere. The maples are red; the poplars are yellow; the oaks are orange. When viewed from a distance, the splash of color is breathtaking. The cats dart into the house and curl up by the wood stove, and the dogs need little excuse to chase each other around the yard. The bright orange pumpkins that grew so big and round beneath the rustling cornstalks have taken their places in the bay windows. Raggedy Ann is lounging near the pumpkin that has been chosen to be this year's jack-o-lantern. The basket of red apples is on the porch by the rocking chair, and the kettle of green tomatoes is in the kitchen. The aroma of the green tomatoes being made into marmalade permeates through the house. James Whitcomb Riley ("When the Frost Is on the Punkin") and Washington Irving ("The Legend of Sleepy Hollow") await their annual visit. When Holly, my good and faithful dog, and I take our evening walk, we can hear Frank's saw straight ahead and Tom's saw down to the left and Jack's saw nearby as everyone is cutting wood to keep the woodboxes full. As we finish our walk, we can see and smell the smoke curling up from the chimney of the log house. Then as we come in the back door, there is the big woodbox full of wood. It is time to think of baking bread again as the warmth from the black wood stove will make it rise. Brown leaves have fallen all over the paths through the woods. So you see, autumn is here. If all the above is not enough, the geese honking in the big, blue sky prove the point.

Sandra Griffith Blake
Townsend, Delaware

Editor's Note: Do you have a special holiday or seasonal memory that you'd like to share with the Ideals family of readers? We'd love to read it! Send your typed memory to:

MY FAVORITE MEMORY
C/O EDITORIAL DEPARTMENT
IDEALS MAGAZINE
535 METROPLEX DRIVE, SUITE 250
NASHVILLE, TENNESSEE 37211

MONARCH BUTTERFLY ON COPPER-COLORED MUMS. Missouri. Gay Bumgarner Photography.

Autumn

Beverly J. Anderson

Amber, crimson, russet, gold—
Foliage colors now unfold.
Bright the sky and crisp the air—
Signs of autumn everywhere.

Orange pumpkins in the field,
Harvest shows a lavish yield.
Roadside stands are quite a treat,
Laden with good things to eat.

Scarlet sumac is ablaze
All along the country ways;
Goldenrod and asters too
Lend their charm for us to view.

Autumn calls the heart to praise
For the bounty of fall days,
For the beauty we behold
When the leaves turn red and gold.

Last Dance

Beverly J. Anderson

The autumn leaves come tumbling down
In yellow, orange, red, and brown.
They skip and waltz and gently glide
As on the crispy breeze they ride.

We watch with joy this autumn day
Their twirling, colorful ballet.
Their merry trip to earth complete,
They make a carpet for our feet.

EASTERN BLACK SWALLOWTAIL ON MAPLE LEAVES. Missouri. Gay Bumgarner Photography.

Autumn's Treasure Chest

Nora M. Bozeman

I'd like to capture autumn's days
When woodlands thick are now ablaze
And golden, harvest, moonlight beams
Shine soft on crimson-colored dreams.

I'd like to capture autumn's air
To give to wintertime to wear.
Then autumn's days of golden glow
Would melt the drifts of silvered snow.

I'd like to capture autumn's crown
Of leaves in red and russet brown
Before her splendor's laid to rest
Inside October's treasure chest.

CASCADING BROOK
Vermont
Gene Ahrens Photography

Readers' Forum

Meet Our Ideals Readers and Their Families

MARK AND MARY ANN BATEMAN of Ogden, Utah, snapped this picture of their son "Little" Mark, then age four, and his friend Rusty, a shelty, taking a break from some summertime outdoor fun. Little Mark is now five years old and has been joined by a brother, Mason, age nine months; but he and Rusty are still best friends.

The Batemans really enjoy receiving *Ideals* and have been subscribing to the magazine for about four years. Dad Mark tells us that his favorite thing about *Ideals* is that "there are no publications that capture the seasons and holidays like yours."

JANE ZORN of Newtown Square, Pennsylvania, says that her granddaughter, six-year-old Samantha Schaffhauser, loves horses. So it was no surprise when Samantha hopped up onto the fence of a corral near Jane's home and instantly made friends with Daisy. Samantha, one of Jane's five grandchildren, is the daughter of Barbara and Rudy Schaffhauser.

Jane has been subscribing to *Ideals* for three years, and she always enjoys sharing the magazine with her family. She first received a subscription to *Ideals* as a birthday present from her daughter.

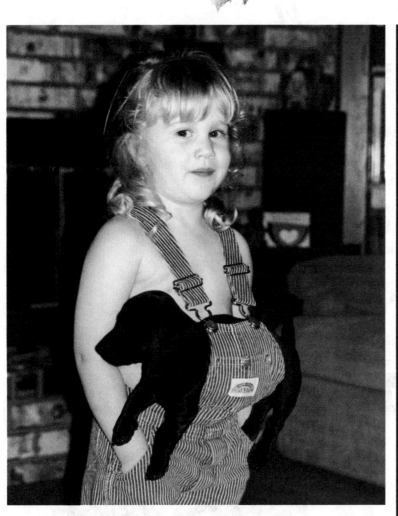

ROSE E. ACTON of Oklahoma City, Oklahoma, sent us this photo of her three-and-a-half-year-old granddaughter Hannah Elizabeth Fuller and a furry friend. Hannah named her new pal "B. D.," which, Rose explains, is short for "Black Dog." Hannah is obviously very proud of B. D., though the originality of his name, Rose admits, is somewhat questionable. In the photo, B. D. is enjoying a ride in the bib of Hannah's overalls. Hannah is one of Rose's seven "very special" grandchildren. She lives with her mom, dad, and older brother Joseph, age eight, in Claremore, Oklahoma.

THANK YOU Mark and Mary Ann Bateman, Jane Zorn, and Rose E. Acton for sharing with *Ideals*. We hope to hear from other readers who would like to share photos and stories with the Ideals family. Please include a self-addressed, stamped envelope if you would like the photos returned. Keep your original photographs for safekeeping and send duplicate photos along with your name, address, and telephone number to:

READERS' FORUM
IDEALS PUBLICATIONS INC.
P.O. BOX 305300
NASHVILLE, TENNESSEE 37230

ideals

Publisher, Patricia A. Pingry
Editor, Lisa C. Ragan
Copy Editor, Michelle Prater Burke
Electronic Prepress, Anne Lesemann
Editorial Assistant, Brian L. Bacon
Editorial Interns, Lara Davies, Connie Flood
Contributing Editors,
Lansing Christman, Deana Deck, Russ Flint,
Pamela Kennedy, Patrick McRae, Mary
Skarmeas, Nancy Skarmeas

ACKNOWLEDGMENTS

UNHARVESTED from *THE POETRY OF ROBERT FROST*, edited by Edward Connery Lathem. Copyright © 1936 by Robert Frost. Copyright © 1969 by Henry Holt and Co., Inc. Reprinted by permission of Henry Holt and Co., Inc. FRIENDSHIP from *THE LIGHT OF FAITH* by Edgar A. Guest, copyright © 1926 by The Reilly & Lee Co. Used by permission of the author's estate. MAKING NEW FRIENDS from *THE WINDING ROAD* by Patience Strong, copyright © 1957 by Patience Strong. Used by permission of Rupert Crew Limited. Excerpt from *CONVERSATIONS WITH AMBER* by Gladys Taber, copyright © 1978 by Gladys Taber. All rights reserved. Reprinted with permission of Brandt & Brandt Literary Agents, Inc.

Loyalty

George L. Ehrman

One can have a loyal friend
and not have wealth
or other things,

But one who has a loyal friend
will have a heart
that always sings!

5-PACK FRIENDSHIP IDEALS

Tell your friends how much they mean to you with a gift of *Friendship Ideals*.

Order now and receive five copies of *Friendship Ideals* for just $20.95 plus $3.50 postage and handling. That's a substantial savings over the newsstand price. Each copy comes with a large greeting envelope to make your gift extra special.

Order number 52170A

Send a check or money order payable to Ideals Publications Inc. to:

Ideals Friendship
P.O. Box 305300
Nashville, TN 37230-5300

For credit card orders, call toll-free:
1-800-558-4343